EASY THAI
STIR-FRIES, SALADS & SIDE DISHES

S

BEEF WITH BROCCOLI AND OYSTER SAUCE

NEAU PAD PAK NAMMAUN HOY

SERVES 4   **PREPARATION TIME: 10 MINUTES**
COOKING TIME: 7–8 MINUTES

The tenderest beef fillet and the brightest green broccoli make perfect partners. Add a dash of oyster sauce, some garlic, spring onions and a generous amount of seasoning and you have a stunning creation.

200g/7oz **broccoli**, cut into tiny florets

400g/14oz **beef** fillet, sliced into neat, even-sized pieces

2 **garlic** cloves, crushed

2 tbsp **oyster sauce**

5 tbsp **chicken stock**

salt and freshly ground **black pepper**

5 **spring onions**, cut into short lengths

4 tbsp **sunflower oil**

1 **ASSEMBLE** all the ingredients.

2 **PLUNGE** the broccoli florets into boiling water for 1 minute, then drain and rinse with cold water.

3 **HEAT** a wok, add the oil and, when very hot, toss in the beef and garlic. Stir-fry for 4 minutes until the meat has changed colour and looks tender.

4 **ADD** the blanched broccoli florets, oyster sauce and the stock. Cover and cook over a high heat for 1–2 minutes, stirring once or twice.

5 **TASTE** for seasoning, toss in the spring onions and stir-fry for a few more seconds.

6 **SERVE** immediately on a hot serving dish.

STIR-FRY NOODLES WITH PORK OR BEEF

GUAY TIEW PAD SI-EW

SERVES 4   PREPARATION TIME: 10 MINUTES
COOKING TIME: 6–8 MINUTES

Rice noodles tossed with stir-fried tender pork or beef fillet, Chinese leaves and delicately scrambled egg, all enhanced with soy and crushed yellow bean sauces and a handful of spring onions – an unbelievable gastronomic experience.

400g/14oz **rice noodles** (*guay tiew*)

2 **garlic** cloves, crushed

225g/8oz **pork** or **beef** fillet, cut into thin strips

1 large **egg**, beaten

6 **Chinese leaves** or any **green leaves**, trimmed and chopped into bite-sized pieces

1 tsp **dark soy sauce**

1 tbsp **light soy sauce**

1 tbsp **crushed yellow bean sauce**

1 tsp **sugar**

salt and freshly ground **black pepper**

4 **spring onions**, cut into neat lengths

2 tbsp **sunflower oil**

1 **SEPARATE** the noodles and plunge into boiling water. Drain, then slice the folded noodles into ribbons.

2 **ASSEMBLE** the remaining ingredients.

3 **HEAT** a wok, add the oil and, when hot, fry the garlic until turning golden, then add the beef or pork and toss all the time until the meat changes colour and is cooked. This will take just a couple of minutes for beef and a little longer for pork.

4 **ADD** the egg to the wok and stir until it just begins to scramble, then add the Chinese or other leaves. Cook for only a few seconds, then add the rice noodles.

5 **TOSS** well and then add the soy sauces, crushed yellow bean sauce and sugar. Mix well and taste for seasoning. Add most of the spring onions.

6 **TURN** into a warmed serving bowl and garnish with the remaining spring onions. Serve immediately.

STIR-FRY PORK AND PRAWNS WITH WING BEANS *MOO LAE GOONG PAD TAO*

**SERVES 4   PREPARATION TIME: 8–10 MINUTES
COOKING TIME: 10 MINUTES**

A fabulous mixture of tender pork tossed in a red curry paste with bright green wing beans and fresh prawns moistened with fish sauce and sweetened to just the right degree.

250g/9oz **wing** or **French beans**, cut into 2.5cm/1in lengths

2 tbsp **red curry paste** *(see page 39)*

225g/8oz **pork** fillet, thinly sliced

3–4 tbsp hot **water**

4 tbsp **fish sauce**

115g/4oz/½ cup peeled cooked **prawns**

1 tbsp **light brown sugar**

4 tbsp **sunflower oil**

freshly ground **black pepper**

1 PLUNGE the beans into boiling water for 2 minutes, then drain, rinse with cold water and drain again.

2 ASSEMBLE the remaining ingredients.

3 HEAT a wok, add the oil and, when hot, stir-fry the curry paste to bring out the flavour. Add the pork slices and cook until the pork changes colour. Thin slices will cook quite quickly.

4 ADD the hot water, fish sauce, prawns and beans. Stir well, then add the sugar and black pepper. Taste and adjust the seasoning, then serve at once.

STIR-FRY CHILLI PORK

MOO PAD PRIK

SERVES **4**   PREPARATION TIME: **10** MINUTES   COOKING TIME: **8** MINUTES

A quick and sumptuous dish of thinly sliced pork fillet, tossed with garlic, chilli and spring onions, moistened with Thai fish sauce and served piping hot. It is important that the pork is sliced very thinly so that it will cook quickly.

400g/14oz **pork** fillet, trimmed and sliced into neat, even-sized pieces

1 small **onion**, finely sliced

2 **garlic** cloves, crushed

1–2 **red chillies**, seeded and finely sliced

4 **spring onions**, cut into short lengths

4 tbsp **stock** or **water**

1 tbsp **fish sauce**

4 tbsp **sunflower oil**

freshly ground **black pepper**

1 **ASSEMBLE** all the ingredients.

2 **HEAT** a wok, add the oil and, when hot, toss in the pork, onion and garlic. Stir-fry for 5–6 minutes until the pork changes colour and is tender.

3 **ADD** the remaining ingredients and quickly toss together. Taste for seasoning and serve immediately on a hot dish.

STIR-FRY CHICKEN WITH BASIL LEAVES

GAI PAD BAI KAPROW

**SERVES 4   PREPARATION TIME: 12–15 MINUTES
COOKING TIME: 8 MINUTES**

The chicken is wonderfully perfumed with fresh basil leaves, but the bird's eye chillies add dragon-like fire. To be truly authentic, the fiendishly hot chillies should be simply crushed, but you may prefer to remove some of the seeds.

---

1 small, finger-length red **chilli**, to garnish

2 **chicken** breasts (175–200g/6–7oz each), boned and skinned and cut into neat, bite-sized pieces

2 **garlic** cloves, crushed

1 **onion**, finely sliced

15 **holy basil leaves**

2–3 **bird's eye chillies**, seeded, if liked, and sliced or crushed

2 tbsp **fish sauce**

1 tsp **light brown sugar**

4 tbsp **sunflower oil**

1 **MAKE** a chilli flower. Slit the top two-thirds of the chilli into fine strips, scraping away the seeds if wished. Leave it to soak in iced water (to speed up the curling process) while you prepare and cook the stir-fry.

2 **ASSEMBLE** all the ingredients.

3 **HEAT** a wok, add half the oil and, when hot, stir-fry the chicken pieces and garlic together. Stir-fry until the chicken pieces change colour and are cooked through. Remove from the wok and keep warm.

4 **WIPE** the wok with kitchen paper, then add the remaining oil and stir-fry the onion with most of the basil leaves and chillies for 3 minutes.

5 **RETURN** the chicken to the wok, add the fish sauce and sugar and mix well.

6 **TURN** on to a hot serving dish and garnish with the chilli flower and remaining basil leaves. Serve at once.

STIR-FRY DUCK BREASTS WITH GINGER AND BLACK BEAN SAUCE *PED PAD KHING*

SERVES 4   PREPARATION TIME: 15 MINUTES
COOKING TIME: 8 MINUTES, PLUS 1 HOUR RENDERING TIME

Another winning combination – fresh root ginger, black bean sauce, garlic and Chinese mushrooms stir-fried with juicy slices of duck breast and spring onions and served garnished with shreds of crispy duck skin.

2 boneless **duck** breasts (280–325g/10–11oz each), finely sliced

6 **Chinese mushrooms**

1 **garlic** clove, crushed

2.5cm/1in piece fresh **ginger**, peeled and shredded

1 small **onion**, sliced

1–2 tbsp **black bean sauce**

1 tsp **sugar**

freshly ground **black pepper**

4 **spring onions**, cut into short lengths

3 tbsp **sunflower oil** or **duck fat** (optional)

1 **PREHEAT** the oven to 180°C/350°F/Gas 4.

2 **TRIM** the skin from the duck breasts, if liked, and render down in an ovenproof dish in the oven for about 1 hour until all the fat has melted and the skin is crisp. Reserve the duck fat for cooking the meat, if wanted, and slice the crisp skin into fine strips for the garnish. Meanwhile, soak the Chinese mushrooms in warm water for 20–30 minutes.

3 **ASSEMBLE** all the remaining ingredients.

4 **DRAIN** the mushrooms, reserving 2–3 tbsp of the soaking liquid. Discard the stalks and slice the mushroom caps finely.

5 **HEAT** the oil or duck fat in a wok and, when hot, add the duck slices, garlic and ginger and toss constantly until the duck meat changes colour and is tender.

6 **ADD** the onion, mushrooms, black bean sauce, sugar and the mushroom soaking liquid. Toss well and taste for seasoning.

7 **ADD** the spring onions and turn out immediately on to a hot serving dish. Serve scattered with the crispy skin slices, if liked.

STIR-FRY CHICKEN WITH CASHEW NUTS

GAI PAD MAMAUNG HIMMAPARN

SERVES 4 **PREPARATION TIME: 12–15 MINUTES**
COOKING TIME: 6 MINUTES

A favourite combination of sweet, almost creamy, cashews roasted to bring out their nuttiness and stir-fried with the tenderest chicken breasts, subtly flavoured with fish and oyster sauces and just a hint of garlic.

2 skinless **chicken** breasts (225g/8oz each), sliced into neat, even-sized strips

1 **garlic** clove, crushed

1 **onion**, finely sliced

55g/2oz/generous ⅓ cup roasted **cashew nuts**, halved lengthways

3 tbsp **fish sauce**

1 tbsp **oyster sauce**

4 **spring onions**, cut into short lengths

salt and freshly ground **black pepper**

3 tbsp **sunflower oil**

1 **ASSEMBLE** all the ingredients.

2 **HEAT** a wok, add the oil and, when hot, toss in the chicken and garlic and stir-fry for 3–4 minutes until the chicken pieces are tender and golden.

3 **ADD** the remaining ingredients. Cook for only 1 minute, then taste for seasoning and serve on a hot serving dish.

SWEET AND SOUR CHICKEN

PAD PRIEW-WAAN GAI

SERVES 4   PREPARATION TIME: 15 MINUTES
COOKING TIME: 8–10 MINUTES

Nothing like Chinese sweet and sour dishes, here the chicken is stir-fried gently then simmered with colourful red and green vegetables, flavoured with tomato, sharpened with rice vinegar and sweetened with sugar to form a rich-tasting sauce.

2 skinless **chicken** breasts (225g/8oz each), sliced into neat, even-sized strips

¼ small **onion**, finely sliced

¼ each **red** and **green pepper**, finely sliced

2.5cm/1in piece **cucumber**, finely sliced

4 **cherry tomatoes**, halved

4 **spring onions**, cut into short lengths

1 tsp **tomato purée**

1 tbsp **rice vinegar**

1 tbsp **fish sauce**

1 tsp **sugar**

4 tbsp **chicken stock** (optional)

4 tbsp **sunflower oil**

freshly ground **black pepper**

coriander leaves, to garnish

1 **ASSEMBLE** all the ingredients.

2 **HEAT** a wok, add the oil and, when hot, stir-fry the chicken pieces for 3–5 minutes until they change colour and are tender.

3 **ADD** all the other ingredients along with the stock, if needed, to make a sauce. Cook for 3–4 minutes. Taste and adjust the seasoning.

4 **SERVE** on a warm dish garnished with coriander leaves.

STIR-FRY SQUID WITH GARLIC

PLA MEUK KRATIEM PRIKTHAI

SERVES 4   PREPARATION TIME: 20 MINUTES   COOKING TIME: 5 MINUTES

As the attractively prepared squid is stir-fried with garlic, coriander, freshly ground black pepper and oyster sauce, the juices give off a heady aroma.

450g/1lb ready-cleaned **squid**

2 tbsp **sunflower oil**

1–2 **garlic** cloves, crushed

2 **coriander** stems, stalks pounded

½ tsp freshly ground **black pepper**

1 tbsp **oyster sauce**

6 **spring onions**, cut into 2.5cm/1in lengths

1 **PREPARE** the squid. If using frozen squid, thaw thoroughly, then pull out the tentacles from each pocket when sufficiently thawed. Slit down the side of each pocket and open it out. Score the inner surface lightly with the back of a knife and cut each one into strips (the scoring helps the sauce to permeate the flesh, but if you wish you can save time by simply cutting any smaller squid into rings). Do not discard the tentacles, which are usually tucked into each ready-cleaned squid – add them to the recipe.

2 **ASSEMBLE** all the ingredients.

3 **HEAT** a wok, add the oil, and, when hot, quickly fry the garlic and pounded coriander stalks (reserving the leaves for the garnish) to bring out the flavour.

4 **KEEP** the wok over a high heat, then add the squid and tentacles. Stir-fry quickly for 2–3 minutes.

5 **ADD** the pepper and oyster sauce and finally the spring onions.

6 **TURN** on to a hot serving dish and serve garnished with the reserved coriander leaves.

STIR-FRY SCALLOPS WITH CHILLI AND BASIL LEAVES *HOY SHELL PAD BAI KAPROW*

SERVES 3–4   PREPARATION TIME: 10 MINUTES
COOKING TIME: 2–3 MINUTES

Scallops stir-fried with onion, chilli, basil and fish sauce create a sensational dish. Scallops are best cooked briefly, and so are highly suited to a stir-fry.

6–8 large **scallops** or about 450g/1lb **queen scallops**

½ **onion**, finely sliced

1 large **red** or **green chilli**, seeded and finely sliced

2 **holy basil** sprigs, leaves only

4 **spring onions**, cut into short lengths

2 tbsp **fish sauce**

1 tsp **sugar**

freshly ground **black pepper**

3 tbsp **sunflower oil**

1 **CUT** the large scallops horizontally through the centre to make two even-sized round shapes. Remove the black thread from the smaller queen scallops and leave whole. Place on kitchen paper to drain any excess moisture.

2 **ASSEMBLE** all the other ingredients. When ready to cook, heat a wok, add the oil and, when hot, toss in the scallops and stir-fry for 1 minute.

3 **PUSH** the scallops to one side, then add the onion to the wok with the chilli and basil leaves. Keep tossing, then add the spring onions, fish sauce, sugar and pepper.

4 **TASTE** and adjust the seasoning, then serve immediately on a hot serving dish.

THAI BEEF SALAD *YUM NEAU*

**SERVES 4   PREPARATION TIME: 15–20 MINUTES
COOKING TIME: 4–6 MINUTES**

Beef fillet, perfectly cooked to a delicate pink, then cut into wafer-thin slices, tossed with matchsticks of carrot and cucumber, thinly sliced red onion, spring onions and a tangy yet fiery dressing, garnished with mint and coriander.

225g/8oz **beef** fillet

salt and freshly ground **black pepper**

3 tbsp **fish sauce**

juice of 1 large **lime** or **lemon**

1 tbsp **sugar**

1 **red chilli**, seeded and finely sliced

4 **shallots** or 1 small **red onion**, finely sliced

2 **garlic** cloves, crushed

2 **lemon grass** stems, lower 5cm/2in finely sliced

⅓ **cucumber**, cut into matchsticks or coarsely grated

2 **carrots**, cut into matchsticks or coarsely grated

2–3 **spring onions**, finely shredded

1 small handful each **coriander** and **mint leaves**

1 **SEASON** the beef, then place it under a hot grill. Cook to medium-rare (about 4–6 minutes, depending on thickness), turning twice during cooking. Allow to rest for 10 minutes before slicing thinly.

2 **BLEND** the fish sauce with the lime or lemon juice, sugar, chilli and half the shallots or onion to make the dressing.

3 **TOSS** the beef slices with the garlic, lemon grass slices, remaining shallots or onion, cucumber, carrots, some of the spring onions and some of the coriander and torn mint leaves. Add the dressing.

4 **PILE** on to a deep serving dish and garnish with the remaining spring onion, coriander and mint leaves. (If this salad is to be eaten as part of a picnic, dress with just a third of the dressing and take the remainder with you to pour over at the last minute.)

THANYING SALAD *YUM THANYING*

SERVES 4 PREPARATION TIME: 30 MINUTES COOKING TIME: 4 MINUTES

Reputed to be a dish revered by the Thai royal family, this mixture of chicken and vegetables folded into a sour, sweet and salty cucumber relish is certainly fit for a king! This is a speciality from a famous restaurant in Bangkok, The Thanying.

¼ **cucumber**, halved, seeded, then coarsely grated or diced

4 **shallots** or 1 small **red onion**, sliced

2–3 **red chillies**, seeded and sliced

2 tbsp **light** or **dark brown sugar**

4 tbsp **rice vinegar**

freshly ground **black pepper**

200g/7oz **long** or **green beans**, trimmed

2 tsp **sesame seeds**, to garnish

55g/2oz/⅓ cup salted **peanuts**, finely crushed

375g/13oz cold cooked **chicken**, cut into fine strips

3 **carrots**, cut into matchsticks

115g/4oz/1 cup **bean sprouts**, brown tails removed if necessary

lettuce leaves, to garnish

6 **coriander stems**, leaves chopped, to garnish

1 **PLACE** the grated or diced cucumber in a bowl. Pound the shallots or onion and chilli to a paste using a pestle and mortar, then add the sugar, vinegar and pepper. It should taste sour, sweet and salty.

2 **PLUNGE** the beans into a saucepan of boiling water for 2 minutes, then drain and cut into pieces.

3 **WARM** a frying pan, then dry-fry the sesame seeds for 2 minutes until golden, moving them all the time to avoid catching.

4 **TOSS** the cucumber and the pounded ingredients together with the peanuts, then fold in the chicken strips, beans, carrots and bean sprouts just before serving.

5 **TURN** on to a serving dish with some lettuce leaves and garnish with coriander leaves and the toasted sesame seeds.

MARKET SALAD *SOM TAM*

SERVES 4   PREPARATION TIME: 15–20 MINUTES

A traditional salad of coarsely grated green papaya and tomato wedges mixed with green beans, fresh red chilli, lemon or lime juice, fish sauce and pounded dried prawns. If green papaya is unavailable, use white cabbage or carrot.

450g/1lb **green papaya**, peeled, or **white cabbage**, shredded, and **carrot**, grated (optional)

1 **red chilli**, seeded and sliced

1–2 **long beans**, sliced, or 6 **green beans**

1 tsp **sugar**

4 tbsp **fish sauce**

juice of 1 **lemon** or **lime**

25g/1oz **dried prawns**, pounded to a powder using a pestle and mortar

2 **tomatoes**, cut into eighths, or 8 **cherry tomatoes**, cut in half

25–55g/1–2oz/¼–⅓ cup **peanuts**, crushed, to garnish

1–2 handfuls **coriander leaves**, chopped, to garnish

1 **HOLD** the papaya in one hand and make deep slim cuts down into the flesh on one side with a very sharp knife. Then take off thin slices lengthways, leaving you with consistently sized shreds. Repeat all the way around on the other side.

2 **CRUSH** the chilli lightly with the beans and sugar using a pestle and mortar, then add the fish sauce and lemon or lime juice to taste.

3 **PLACE** the powdered dried prawns, tomatoes, papaya or cabbage (or a mixture of cabbage and carrot) in a bowl, add the crushed chilli mixture and toss lightly.

4 **TURN** on to a serving dish. Top with the peanuts and coriander leaves just before serving.

GREEN MANGO SALAD

YUM MA-MAUNG

SERVES 4   PREPARATION TIME: 15 MINUTES
COOKING TIME: 1–2 MINUTES

A stunning layered salad of tart green mangoes, dried prawns, toasted coconut and finely sliced red onion, on a lettuce-lined dish, drizzled with a spicy sweet and sour dressing and garnished with mint or coriander leaves.

---

2 large **green mangoes** or hard unripe **yellow mangoes** (these will give a sweeter result) or 1 **pomelo** or **grapefruit**

55g/2oz/½ cup **desiccated coconut**

soft **lettuce**

55g/2oz **dried prawns**, pounded to a powder using a pestle and mortar

1 **red onion**, finely sliced

mint leaves, torn, or **coriander leaves**

DRESSING:

juice of 1 large **lime** or ½ **lemon**

3 tbsp **fish sauce**

1–2 **bird's eye chillies** (or more), seeded and finely sliced

2 tbsp **dark brown sugar**

1 PEEL the mangoes with a potato peeler. Holding one in the palm of your hand, use a sharp knife to make lots of close cuts in the flesh of the mango. Now slice through the close cuts to make fine shards of flesh and repeat on the other side. Repeat with the second mango. If using a pomelo or grapefruit, remove the skin, divide into segments and remove the membranes, then chop lightly.

2 WARM a frying pan, then dry-fry the coconut for 1–2 minutes until golden, keeping it on the move to prevent it catching.

3 BLEND together the dressing ingredients in a jug.

4 LINE a serving dish with lettuce leaves then layer up the mango, powdered prawns, coconut and onion and some of the coriander or torn mint leaves.

5 POUR the dressing over the salad and garnish with the remaining coriander or torn mint. Toss before each person takes their helping.

BABY CORN AND SUGAR SNAPS WITH GINGER AND GARLIC *PAD YOD KAO POD KAB KHING*

SERVES 4   PREPARATION TIME: 6–8 MINUTES   COOKING TIME: 5 MINUTES

Vibrantly coloured vegetables with zingy ginger and garlic flavours, which can be cooked and served in double-quick time. The oyster sauce adds a gloss and sophistication to these simple vegetables.

4 **garlic** cloves, sliced

2.5cm/1in piece fresh **ginger**, peeled and cut into matchsticks

½ **onion**, finely sliced

115g/4oz **baby sweetcorn**, cut in half at an angle

115g/4oz **sugar snap peas**

1 tbsp **oyster sauce**

1 tbsp **fish sauce**

1 tbsp boiling **water**

2 tbsp **sunflower oil**

freshly ground **black pepper**

1 **ASSEMBLE** all the prepared vegetables next to the stove.

2 **BLEND** the oyster and fish sauces with the water in a bowl.

3 **HEAT** a wok before adding the oil. Allow to become hot, then toss in the garlic, ginger and onion, turning all the time so that the garlic does not brown and become bitter.

4 **ADD** the sweetcorn and sugar snap peas and toss well for 2 minutes then pour in the sauce mixture. Cover with a lid and cook for 1 minute.

5 **TOP** with a little black pepper and serve on a warm serving dish.

MIXED STIR-FRY VEGETABLES

PAD PAK RUAM MITR

SERVES 4   PREPARATION TIME: 12 MINUTES   COOKING TIME: 5 MINUTES

This deliciously crisp and colourful stir-fry makes the perfect accompaniment to any main dish, or could just be eaten on its own. Choose any vegetables you want, but aim for a good mix of colour and texture for the perfect result.

450g/1lb **mixed vegetables**: broccoli, green beans, Brussels sprouts, carrots, cabbage, bean sprouts and/or spinach (any combination), trimmed and cut into bite-sized pieces

3 tbsp **water**

2 tbsp **fish sauce**

2 tbsp **oyster sauce**

3 tbsp **sunflower oil**

2 **garlic** cloves, finely chopped

½ tsp **sugar**

freshly ground **black pepper**

1 **RINSE** and drain the vegetables. Set the cabbage, bean sprouts and/or spinach aside. Assemble all the vegetables by the stove.

2 **COMBINE** the water, fish and oyster sauces in a small bowl.

3 **HEAT** a wok, add the oil and first fry the garlic without browning it too much.

4 **ADD** all the remaining vegetables, except for the cabbage, bean sprouts and/or spinach, then add the sugar and season with black pepper. Toss well, turning all the time to cook while retaining the crunchiness.

5 **ADD** the sauce mixture and the remaining vegetables. Reduce the heat, cover and cook for a further 2 minutes.

6 **SERVE** on a warm serving dish.

SPICY GREEN BEANS

PAD PED TOU KAG

SERVES **4**   PREPARATION TIME: **6–8** MINUTES   COOKING TIME: **5** MINUTES

*These beans are a rich vibrant colour and full of flavour and crispness.
The combination of the beans with aromatic curry paste and piquant
fish sauce creates a perfect vegetable dish for any Thai meal.*

450g/1lb **green** or **long beans**, stalk end trimmed, and sliced into 5cm/2in pieces

3 tbsp **sunflower oil**

1 tbsp **red curry paste** *(see page 39)*

2 tbsp **fish sauce**

2 tbsp **sugar**

125ml/4fl oz/½ cup boiling **water**

1 **PLUNGE** the beans into a saucepan of boiling water for 30 seconds, then drain and set aside.

2 **HEAT** a wok, add the oil and swirl it over the surface of the pan. Add the curry paste, then fry over a moderate heat until it changes colour and gives off a rich, fragrant aroma.

3 **ADD** the green beans and stir-fry until they are tender. Add the fish sauce, sugar and water and bring the mixture rapidly to the boil.

4 **TRANSFER** the cooked beans and sauce to a warm serving bowl and serve immediately.

STIR-FRY GREEN VEGETABLES WITH YELLOW BEAN SAUCE *PAT PAK BOONG FAI DAENG*

SERVES 4   PREPARATION TIME: 5 MINUTES   COOKING TIME: 3—4 MINUTES

Oriental greens stir-fried with a glorious mixture of crushed yellow bean sauce, garlic and chillies. If you cannot buy pak boong, baby spinach makes a perfect substitute. Alternatively, use a combination of pak choy and Savoy cabbage.

1–2 **chillies**, seeded and finely chopped

3 tbsp **crushed yellow bean sauce**

1 **garlic** clove, crushed

1 tbsp **sugar**

3 tbsp **sunflower oil**

400g/14oz **pak boong** or **young spinach**, or **pak choy**, leaves used whole and white stalks cut into bite-sized pieces, and **Savoy cabbage**, leaves torn

1 **PLACE** the chopped chillies, crushed yellow bean sauce, garlic and sugar in a bowl.

2 **HEAT** a wok, add the oil and, when hot, toss in the spicy sauce and the green vegetables together. Stir-fry for 3—4 minutes.

3 **TURN** on to a hot plate and serve at once.

RICE

PLAIN BOILED RICE

KHAO TOM

**SERVES 4   PREPARATION TIME: 2 MINUTES
COOKING TIME: 12–15 MINUTES**

1 **WASH** 225g/8oz/1 cup rice thoroughly in several changes of water until the water looks clear, to remove the starch.

2 **PLACE** the rice in a heavy-based saucepan with 500ml/17fl oz/generous 2 cups water and bring to the boil. Reduce the heat, stir, cover the pan and simmer for 12–15 minutes.

3 **REMOVE** the lid and stir with a chopstick or fork.

4 **USE** at once or transfer to a serving bowl, three-quarters covered with clingfilm, and microwave on full power for 4 minutes in 650w microwave or 3 minutes in 900w just before serving. Alternatively, place in an oiled steamer, cover with a lid and set over a saucepan of gently bubbling water for 8–10 minutes until well heated through. Stir with a chopstick to prevent breaking up the grains.

STEAMED RICE *KHAO SUAY*

**SERVES 3–4   PREPARATION TIME: 3 MINUTES
COOKING TIME: 25 MINUTES**

225g/8oz/1 cup **Thai fragrant rice**

600ml/21fl oz/2½ cups **water**

½ tsp **salt**

oil, for brushing

1 **PLACE** the rice in a sieve or a bowl and rinse thoroughly.

2 **BOIL** the water and salt in a heavy-based saucepan. Stir in the rice.

3 **RETURN** to the boil and stir once or twice to prevent the rice settling on the saucepan bottom. Cook uncovered over a medium heat until the water has been absorbed, about 6–8 minutes, and the surface is covered in tiny crater-like holes.

4 **BRUSH** the base of the steamer lightly with oil. If it has large holes, cover with either a muslin cloth or some foil that has been punctured with several holes to allow the steam to cook the rice. Drain the rice in a sieve or colander.

5 **TRANSFER** the rice into the steamer; make a few holes in the rice with a chopstick so that the steam can circulate. Set the steamer over a saucepan of boiling water. Cover with the lid and allow to cook for 15 minutes, when the rice will be fluffy and ready to serve. Top up with boiling water as needed.

6 **FORK** through with a roasting fork or chopstick. The rice can be cooked an hour or more ahead of the meal and reheated as for boiled rice (see left).

PASTES

RED CURRY PASTE

KRUENG GAENG PHED

MAKES **375g/13oz** PREPARATION TIME: **30–35** MINUTES
COOKING TIME: **2–3** MINUTES

10 **red chillies**, seeded and sliced

115g/4oz **red onions** or **shallots**, sliced

4 **garlic** cloves, sliced

3 **lemon grass** stems, lower stem only, sliced and bruised

1cm/½in piece **kha**, peeled and sliced

4 **coriander** stems, stalks and roots only

1–2 tbsp **sunflower oil**

1 tsp grated **magrut**

1cm/½in cube prepared **kapi**

1 tbsp **coriander seeds**

2 tsp **cumin seeds**

8–10 **black peppercorns**

1 tsp **salt**

1 **BLEND** the chillies, onions or shallots, garlic, lemon grass, kha and coriander to a fine paste with the oil in a food processor. Add the magrut and prepared kapi.

2 **DRY-FRY** the seeds for a few minutes, then grind to a powder with the peppercorns using a pestle and mortar. Add to the paste with the salt. Blend well. Spoon into a glass jar, cover with clingfilm and a tight-fitting lid and refrigerate.

GREEN CURRY PASTE

GAENG KHIEW WAAN

MAKES **325g/11oz** PREPARATION TIME: **30–35** MINUTES
COOKING TIME: **2–3** MINUTES

10 **green chillies**, seeded and sliced

115g/4oz **white onions** or **shallots**, sliced

4 **garlic** cloves, sliced

3 **lemon grass** stems, lower stem only, sliced and bruised

1cm/½in piece **kha**, peeled and sliced

4 **coriander** stems, leaves, stalks and roots

4 **lime leaves**, sliced

1–2 tbsp **sunflower oil**

1 tsp grated **magrut**

1cm/½in cube prepared **kapi**

1 tbsp **coriander seeds**

2 tsp **cumin seeds**

8–10 **black peppercorns**

1 tsp **salt**

1 **BLEND** the chillies, onions or shallots, garlic, lemon grass, kha, coriander and lime leaves to a fine paste with the oil in a food processor. Add the magrut and prepared kapi.

2 **DRY-FRY** the seeds for a few minutes, then grind to a powder with the peppercorns using a pestle and mortar. Add to the spice paste with the salt. Store as for red curry paste.

Easy Thai Stir-Fries, Salads & Side Dishes
Sallie Morris

This edition first published in the United Kingdom and Ireland in 2012 by
Siena Books, an imprint of Duncan Baird Publishers Ltd
Sixth Floor, Castle House
75–76 Wells Street
London W1T 3QH

Conceived, created and designed by Duncan Baird Publishers

Managing Editor: Grace Cheetham
Editors: Gillian Haslam and Alison Bolus
Designer: Sailesh Patel
Studio Photography: William Lingwood
Photography Assistant: Alice Deuchar
Stylists: Jenny White (food) and Helen Trent (props)

British Library Cataloguing-in-Publication Data:
A CIP record for this book is available from the British Library

ISBN: 978-1-84899-097-5

10 9 8 7 6 5 4 3 2 1

Typeset in Spectrum and Univers
Colour reproduction by Scanhouse, Malaysia
Printed in China by Imago

Publisher's note
While every care has been taken in compiling the recipes for this book,
Duncan Baird Publishers, or any other persons who have been involved
in working on this publication, cannot accept responsibility for any
errors or omissions, inadvertent or not, that may be found in the recipes
or text, nor for any problems that may arise as a result of preparing one
of these recipes. If you are pregnant or breastfeeding or have any special
dietary requirements or medical conditions, it is advisable to consult a
medical professional before following any of the recipes contained in
this book.

Notes on the recipes
Unless otherwise stated:
- Use medium eggs
- Use fresh herbs
- Do not mix metric and imperial measurements
- 1 tsp = 5ml
  1 tbsp = 15ml
  1 cup = 250ml

Language notes
English and Thai names are used throughout the book. There is no
definitive way to translate spellings from Thai to English because Thai
is tonal. *Nam* can be *nahm*, *phed* can be *phet* and *tom khaa gai* can be *tom ga khai*.
If in doubt, say the word out loud.